I NEVER THOUGHT I WOULD BE A STATISTIC

JOANNE M. CHÉRISMA

I Never Thought I Would Be A Statistic
Surviving Abuse

Copyright ©2018 by Joanne M. Chérisma

All rights reserved. No part of this book may be reproduced, copied, stored or transmitted in any form or by any means – graphic, electronic, or mechanical, including photocopying, recording, or information storage and retrieval systems without the prior written permission of Joanne M. Chérisma or HOV Publishing except where permitted by law.

HOV Publishing a division of HOV, LLC.
www.hovpub.com
hopeofvision@gmail.com

Cover Design: HOV Design Solutions
Interior Images: Google images
Editor: Dianna Knox-Cooper
Proofreader: Katrina McRae

Write the Author Joanne M. Chérisma at:
Email: joannecherisma@hotmail.com

For more information about special discounts for bulk purchases, please contact: joannecherisma@hotmail.com

ISBN 978-1-942871-35-4

Library of Congress Control Number: 9781942871354

10   9   8   7   6   5   4   3   2   1

Printed in the United States of America

For my beloved son
Gabriel

Sale of this book without a front cover may be unauthorized. If the book is coverless, it may have been reported to the publisher as "unsold or destroyed" and neither the author nor the publisher may have received payment for it.

This book is based on a true story.

Visit us on the Web!
https://www.facebook.com/Beyond-the-Abuse-2092353357655937/

ACKNOWLEDGEMENT
SPECIAL THANKS

I am using this opportunity to express my gratitude to my mother Joseline Jeanty, my brother Joseph Michael Chérisma, and all my family members who supported me throughout this journey. I am thankful for their love, advice, and constructive criticism.

A very special thank you to Pastor Liz McCreary for her support, encouragement, and unlimited patience. To Bishop Derrick Farmer and First Lady Janice Farmer and to the whole congregation of CPT, thank you for your kindness, love, counsel, guidance, and teaching.

I express my warm appreciation to Zipporah Colòn for her support and availability and for sharing her pearls of knowledge and understanding with me. She successfully kept me focused during this challenging stage of my life.

To Rosheda L. Honorat, Blondine Jean-Charles, Rosetta Naire, Jennifer Johnson-Arnoux, Adam Skar, Gerty Pompe, Jerry Marcelin, Adana Wellington, Madeline Lund, Katrina Greene, Jonathan McCreary and so many others; thank you for your friendship, availability and invaluable help. Your encourage-ment when times were rough is much appreciated and duly noted. It was a great comfort and relief to know that I could count on you.

Joanne M. Chérisma

TABLE OF CONTENTS

INTRODUCTION…………………………….viii

THE WAIT ………………………………………………1
Poem

CHAPTER 1 …………………………………………….3
Denial
Tic Toc Tic Toc Poem

CHAPTER 2 …………………………………………….9
Broken
Eternity Poem

CHAPTER 3 ……………………………………………17
Torture
Pieces Poem

CHAPTER 4 ……………………………………………26
Debilitated
Their Kind of Love Poem

CHAPTER 5 ……………………………………………38
New Beginning
Twenty-Four Seconds Poem

CHAPTER 6 50
Articles
Why Abused Victims Don't Speak Up?
Children and Domestic Violence
Stop Empowering Abusers
Some Examples of Abusive Situations

ABOUT THE AUTHOR 66
JOURNAL 68

I NEVER THOUGHT I WOULD BE A STATISTIC

INTRODUCTION

Growing up we all have dreams and aspirations. For some of us, our parents make sure that we always have the best of everything. They do their very best to make sure that we do not suffer from any lack. From our birth to adulthood; from our first day of school to our graduation; from the day they bring us home from the hospital to our wedding day; our parents want to believe in the idea of us being safe, happy and in peace.

Sometimes the danger we must fear the most are the dangers found within one's own family, friends, co-workers, and even spouses. These are the people in whom we put our trust in the most. These are also the very same people we'd like to believe are supposed to protect us. But some of these people represent the many faces of our suffering and pain. They are the face of our abusers.

I Never Thought I Would Be A Statistic

Based on statistics from the Safe Horizon website, the largest non-profit victim services agency in the United States:

- Women ages 18 to 34 are at greatest risk of becoming victims of domestic violence.

- More than 4 million women experience physical assault and rape by their partners.

- In 2 out of 3 female homicide cases, females are killed by a family member or intimate partner.

Who would have thought that 20 years ago I would be part of those numbers today?

My name is J'Mae and this is my story…

The Wait

I am sitting at that intersection hoping
That you will soon make up your mind
Will you stay
Or will you go away

Eagerly impatient for something to happen
I am anticipating
Been down that valley before
I know the ending

But some part of me just can't seem to break the cycle
For so long I have been praying the wrong prayers
And wanting the wrong things
Then suddenly out of nowhere you appeared

I offered you my heart
It was not enough
I opened my mind
It was not sufficient

And at that interval, I am just wondering

I Never Thought I Would Be A Statistic

How long will I be sitting there?
Because enslaved of my own self
I don't seem to be able to move on.

CHAPTER 1

Denial

As a child, I was taught that once you do good, good will come back to you. My mother did her best to make sure that my brother and I were not exposed to any situation that would harm us. We were supposed to be the best children possible, go to school, fulfill all that was required of us, and become good citizens. This plan, however, was soon diverted as we started to meet different kinds of people in our lives. In 2010, a catastrophic earthquake erupted in my country. Hundreds of people lost their lives during that tragedy, but I survived.

This event shifted my life in a way that I would have never expected. I was injured and in a coma for eleven days. I almost died. I truly thought that nothing worse could ever happen in my life. I was wrong. No loss or tragedy of my past could ever compare to the physical, verbal, and emotional abuse I would suffer in my marriage.

Have you ever been in so much pain that you thought dying would be the easiest way out? Have you ever felt so low and disgusting that you thought that nothing could ever make you whole or clean again? Have you ever been so lost in your mind that even thinking felt like an impossible task? You just want to lay down right there, day after day after day. Your actions become just a repetition of movement and you are simply going through the motion. Somehow you manage to do everything that is expected from you, but deep inside you have just become numb; numb to the pain, numb to the hurt, numb to life.

For more than five years, I have been numb. So numb, that I lost count. All I knew to do was to try and make the best of my situation. You may have asked yourself, "How can someone stay in any inhuman situation?" Well, at some point of my life, I remembered asking myself the same question. I just never thought I would be a statistic. I would lie to myself saying such things as: *I am certainly not a victim. He will get better. I can change him. Maybe if I stay quiet long enough he will stop screaming and then maybe I can fall asleep. In the morning, I woud realize that it was all just a nightmare.* But soon my nightmares became my day mares. Even, when I found out he cheated; I still thought that I could make the best of this situation. *My son needs his father*, I would tell myself.

I cried many tears and suffered heartbreak after heartbreak. My days began to look gloomy as I felt myself slipping into depression. I was merely existing day by day. I started repeating motivational quotes and reciting inspirational lines throughout the day. I was trying to make those truths my reality, but I was just lying to myself.

Tic Toc Tic Toc

Tic toc tic toc
Clock clicking
Heart biting
Tic toc tic toc

Tic toc tic toc
Voice whispering
Heart sighing
Tic toc tic toc

Tic toc tic toc
Tears falling
Heart breaking
Tic toc tic toc

I Never Thought I Would Be A Statistic

Tic toc tic toc
Eyes closing
Heart stopping
Tic toc tic toc

CHAPTER 2

Broken

I remember the first time he hit me. I was pregnant and unemployed. I thought that without him I would not make it. I thought he was the best thing that ever happened to me. I thought we were having this baby together. I thought we were so tight; I thought we were one. Those were the lies I believed.

It was early one morning, and he was mad from the night before. I must have gone through his phone or questioned him about some girl. Who knows? Whatever it was, "It was not my place," he said. According to him, I had my own issues and insecurities that I needed to take care of. A heated exchange of words soon became yelling and the yelling turned to screaming. The screams brought on rage. It was only a matter of seconds before I found myself knocked to the floor.

"Are you crazy?" I screamed.

"Look what you made me do!" He yelled back.

I screamed to him, "You are crazy!"

He came toward me and angrily said, "I am going to show you crazy!"

The next thing I know, his ice cold hands were closing around my neck. With a terrifying look in his eyes, he squeezed his hands and slowly started cutting off my airway. I could see all the demons in hell in his eyes. Soon, fighting back was not an option anymore, as breathing became impossible and life started leaving my body. My vision blurred, and the room started spinning.

How could I have possibly gotten myself in this situation? Was I that awful of a wife? The numerous *why*'s and *how*'s; even if they did not matter at the moment, were popping into my head. One single tear fell from my eye and rolled down my cheek. He looked at me and let me go.

I tried to catch my breath, as I questioned myself; *Am I dreaming? What just happened?* I sat down and decided to call the cops.

He looked at me and said, "You see what you just did?"

"Did I really do this? How did I do that to myself? How could I have choked myself?" I asked as I held the phone to my ear.

"9-1-1," The voice answered on the other side of the line.

Things blurred again, "Ma'am I am pregnant, and my husband just hit me." My own voice sounded so strange to me and another tear fell from my eye. I was in shock as to what had just happened to me. I could not believe it was real.

He looked at me and fiercely said, "Now you have called the cops, are you satisfied? They are going to take me away and you are going to be raising our son by yourself. Is this what you wanted? Maybe that is what you wanted... Now you want to be quiet, when you had a whole lot to say before? You are unbelievable." And while his lamenting continued, my head kept spinning more and more. Suddenly, there was a knock at the door.

- "Police! Open the door." He opened the door.

I could not believe the look on his face. It bore all the pain in the world and somehow in that moment I felt sympathy for him. All the while realizing I was trapped. Another tear fell.

"Ma'am, are you hurt?" The policeman asked.

"No." I answered.

"Ma'am, do you want to press charges or make a report?" He continued.

"I will make a report, but I do not want him to get arrested." I said with concern in my voice.

After the police left, he said to me "I am leaving you. You are a dangerous unstable woman, and I do not feel safe around you."

I burst into tears. I was thinking. *What just went wrong*? "Didn't I just tell the cops not to arrest you?" I asked him.

He packed some clothes and left the apartment. I tried to pull myself together, but all of the emotions were making my head spin. My chest got tight and I could barely breathe. So, I pulled my pregnant body up off the floor and went to take a shower.

That day was one of the longest, loneliest days of my life. It was cold, sad, and insignificant. Later that night he came back. He brought me flowers, cried, and told me he was sorry. He said it would never happen again. He told me that he loved me so much and that he could not be without me.

Then he cried some more, and I cried too. He kissed me, and as I returned his kiss, I knew I was signing my own death certificate. That night we laid together and I fulfilled my marital duties.

Eternity

Nothing changes
My life, perpetual resumption
Nothing moves
My heart, eternal tearing

Same sighs
Same desires
Same aches
Same scenes

On the horizon, no hope
It's only a long way
A naive song

An intensity that makes you drunk
A sword that kills
A life that is destroyed

CHAPTER 3

Torture

The abuse continued for the next five years. I was so hurt. I began to realize that I was not the same person anymore. My actions did not have any meaning. I was going with the flow. Joy, pain, hurt, happiness, I could not express any feelings. I did not have any. They were all gone. Like a zombie, I was going through the day. Only one soul mattered; my son. I looked at him and I told myself, *I have to stay alive for that child.* I had to make sure he was safe and stayed safe. I was feeling so weak and ashamed. *How did I put myself in such a situation? How did I get there?* Slowly the hurt turned into sadness, the sadness into anger, and the anger into frustration.

Those five years were the longest of my life. He blamed me for everything that happened. He wrote letter after letter and brought cards and flowers. But nothing changed.

And finally, one dark day in October, I found out that he was cheating again. He was telling this woman about us and still blaming and criticizing me. I could not believe it. I think some part of me was really hoping that he was going to change and life with him was going to get better. This situation was the last drop that made the cup run over. I remember getting so upset. I looked up her name in the phone book, found her number and called her. I told her more than I probably should have about him. I exposed his past and his current violent behavior. I did not really care at this point. She seemed to be a bit confused and promised me that he was the one pursuing her. Like I said before, I had gotten to the point where I wasn't concerned about anything regarding him anymore. So, she called him while I was on the phone to prove to me that she was right. And I listened to him telling lies after lies.

When he found out that I was listening on the line, he lost it. He decided that he was moving out. I was relieved. However, the situation soon turned worst when he realized that I had told her about his past and she decided to stay away from him. He came home talking about teaching me a lesson. But this time, I was ready. I was fed up with the situation. I just wanted him to leave. I did not want to deal with him anymore. I was finally ready in my mind. This was the day that I had enough strength to stand up for myself.

We started arguing as soon as he came home. I could not stand this anymore. I just wanted him to leave. He started screaming. I just wanted him to be quiet. He started pushing me. I just wanted this to stop. "Get away from me!" I screamed. He looked at me, smiled and kept pushing me. His face was scrunched up in anger. I told him that I was not scared of him anymore.

"Oh yeah! We are going to see if you are still going to have that much to say in a few minutes B…!" then he started choking me.

At that very moment, my son woke up from his nap and started screaming which distracted him. Taking advantage of that quick second, I ran out on the street and he ran after me. I ran into a convenience store and started asking for help. But the guys there looked at me like I was crazy. I asked for a phone to call the police but they refused.

He arrived at the convenience store a few minutes after me and told the men there that I was trying to get him in trouble because I was upset. They seemed to sympathize with him. They looked at me as if I was a mad woman. "Why would you want to get him in trouble?" one of them asked. "He is a good guy."

Yes, in the eyes of the public it appeared that he was the perfect, outgoing, nice husband, and I was the dramatic, unbalanced and insecure woman who was driving him crazy. He managed to get me back in the house. Then, once we got there, he said to me, "Look what you did! We really had to get that many people in our business?" Then he looked at me and asked, "What do you want?"

I looked up and passively said, "I'd like for you to leave."

And just like that, he said, "Ok."

He stood up, packed up some clothes, put them in a bag, and simply told me he would be back to get the rest of his things later on that week. Then, he left. I was still shaking and scared. I started thinking that I probably needed to change the locks on the doors because he could come back in the middle of the night and kill me. I started sleeping with chairs behind the doors and knives under my pillows. I was having nightmares.

Finally, the locks were changed but I was still afraid. I was afraid to go to work, afraid to go to sleep, afraid that I would one day pick up my son from school and that he would be missing because his father would have tried to take him away from me. Then, one day unexpectedly, he came by the house to get more clothes. Scared, I avoided being in the same room with him.

Everything was going well until he called our son and started to whisper in his ears. I stated that he should not be questioning our son because he was only a child. He looked at me with rage and screamed, "Nobody is going to tell me what to do or not to do with my child!" He rushed toward me and grabbed my wrist with strength and sternly said, "Come here!"

As he began talking to me, I began to think to myself. *No, I can't do this anymore.* I managed to remain calm and just listen to his insignificant speech. He spoke for about thirty minutes, complaining that I was not paying enough attention to him and he left. *I cannot do this anymore;* I kept telling myself that I needed to do something about it.

Pieces

I don't want to live in the past
I don't want to keep thinking about You
I don't want to feel the pain
I don't want to fall into pieces

You and I weren't meant to be
You and I wouldn't survive the storm
You and I weren't strong enough
You and I were just a mirage

My chest hurting
My mind racing
My heart breaking
My tears falling

I Never Thought I Would Be A Statistic

Now I'm falling
Now you're leaving
Now I'm crying
Now I'm dying

Know better!
Be stronger!
Speak louder!

STAY ALONE FOR EVER!

CHAPTER 4

Debilitated

Following that incident, I took all the strength I had left to head to family court where I filed for an order of protection and custody our son. Thus, that long fight in court started in January 2016.

For one year, I had to go back and forth to family court and watch him tell lie after lie, and act like a victim. He portrayed himself to be this awesome father while his awful wife was trying to prevent him from contacting his son. I dealt with so much emotion, and shed many tears, with fear continually gripping my heart. Every time I would step foot in the courtroom, I would pray that it would be the last time. I could not bear the idea that my kid would be raised by that lunatic. This thought in itself gave me all the strength I needed to keep fighting. Seeing him in court so relaxed and unconcerned, was so disturbing to me.

I began to be weary of the whole situation. I was so tired of defending myself and proving that I was a good mother. I was tired of seeing him coming and going without having to pay for his actions. I had had enough of being afraid of him harming me. I was impatient in waiting for the court's decision on the case. And then, the unusual started happening. He started not showing up to the hearing. His lawyer had no idea of what was happening to him. He simply vanished.

After missing about 3 hearings, the judge decided to move forward with the case. In December 2016, the Decision and Final Order on Petition for Custody and Order of Protection was made upon Default. "I shall have SOLE LEGAL AND PHYSICAL CUSTODY of the subject Child…" and he had to completely stay away from us and refrain from any communication by any means for 5 years.

God only knows how much longer the process would have taken if he had not stopped showing up in court. I was just so happy that it was over and that I did not have to lose my son in the process. He deserved a much better life than what he had so far. And I was feeling so guilty. I had learned so much dealing with this situation. One of the most significant lessons that I learned was that you should *Never Stop Encouraging Yourself, You Should Speak What You Seek Until You See What You Have Said*. This is just one thing that you must do for yourself as you live for potential and not in limitation; realizing that your feelings are valid.

After filing for divorce in 2016, my life started taking a different turn. In my head, I knew I didn't want to deal with this situation anymore. But, what I didn't realize was that it was going to be a part of me forever. I was so ashamed of my life for some reason and I was feeling stuck. I was hurt... so hurt; and back then, I just didn't fully understand how little control I had over my life.

I didn't want to ever deal with this man anymore. I didn't want to see him anymore. I was in a quest for brand-new opportunities to rebuild myself, my life and my story. I started looking for ways out of my pain and my suffering. And for a while, I thought getting divorced was the way. I thought the sooner that process started, the sooner it would be over. But it was not the case.

It was just another ending point in my life, another failure, another disappointment, another reminder of the fantasy life I had created in my head. Every day, I would remind myself of all the good reasons why I was built for this life and why I needed to keep moving, but the truth deep inside was that I was weakening. I kept repeating to myself, "I can do all things through Christ which strengthened me."

At some point, I started feeling trapped, broken, sad, alone, and misunderstood. It was like I was watching my life from outside of my body. And through all my emotional pain, my silence became golden.

All the disappointments and all my unseen scars were taking over my life. I knew it was getting bad when I started questioning the reasons I was still alive. Have you ever been in so much pain that even breathing become almost impossible? I knew then I needed to get out. I literally felt life coming out of my body. I started feeling ashamed of my life and of myself. I was tired of that vicious cycle I could not seem to get out of. I did not want nor; did I like what I was becoming. I did not want my son to be part of that. I started to put on a facade, a show, a fake smile that made everyone think I was getting better. I pretended that I had things under control, but deep inside these dark thoughts were coming back. I wanted to be somebody else. Once again, I wanted to disappear. I was broken because I believed I was an imperfect soul.

I wanted to have that light shining through my eyes, but inside they were just sad and lifeless. I thought that I would get better with time… yet that wasn't the case. Then, one night the thought finally came back in its complete fruition. I was contemplating an idea. I was enjoying it. I wanted to commit suicide.

At that moment, to me, it was the only way out; it was the fastest way out, the easiest way out. I have been on that road before. I knew the signs, but I had never said it out loud until now… "Maybe I should kill myself." Then I turned around and I saw my son, my family and my students peacefully laying down next to me. I felt horrible and repulsive. *How could I let myself go back that low? How could I be so weak?* Suddenly, my dried eyes weren't so dry anymore. *I needed a different way out. I needed to get out. I needed help.*

I was not going to give up. For my son's sake, I could not give up. I needed to find the patience and the strength to continue. I had to find hope; I had to believe in the future. I needed to believe that a new beginning was possible. I needed God. I needed Jesus. Finally, on February 16, 2017, I was able to get saved. I accepted the Lord Jesus Christ as my personal Savior. I decided then to believe in that Higher Power and allow myself to be led by Him totally. I decided to believe that He was in control and that without Him, I was not anything. I decided to believe that everything I was going through was for a greater purpose. I decided to focus, not so much on the pain, but more so on the walk through the pain. I realized that it was my pain that got me healed. The interesting fact about hitting rock bottom is there is only one way to go... UP. Then, out of nowhere, my life made so much more sense. I would no longer have to sacrifice my dignity for my destiny. The hardest part was over. I was walking away. The choice was way simpler than it was all those years before. Slowly, but surely, I started to rise up; I began to embrace my past and walk into my destiny.

For a long time, I had been relying on people. Most of the time, almost 99 percent of the time I would get disappointed, hurt, judged, or put in a certain category and taken advantage of. They would look at me and automatically envision my story. I would break down and perpetuate the same cycle. Somehow, I always felt that I needed that close human presence to remain alive. I needed to belong. I needed to be attached to something or somebody to be strong.

Then, I realized that for the most part of my life it had only been me and… Jesus. As much as people say they love you, once they go into survival mode, you do not really matter as much. So, why should I put myself in the predicament to always go back to the pain if I already knew how the story will end? If I say that God is my all, why not really treat Him as such? Why not put ALL my trust in HIM? If I really believe "He did it before He will do it again," why am I so worried about life? If I know He lives in me, why not rely on that Power and that Strength that's already within me?

Yes, my friend, I am stronger than I think I am.

I Never Thought I Would Be A Statistic

I was learning how to finally stand alone. I was getting that freedom. I decided to let go. I would no longer be bound from that situation. I was set free and ready to move on…

Their Kind of Love

When they love you so much that as soon as time
gets hard you become expedient
When they love you so much that they do not
hesitate to make you feel like a parasite
When they love you so much that they can't help
themselves looking down on you

When they love you so much that your feelings only
matter when you are part of the clique
When they love you so much that is their way
or no way
When they love you so much that you become
their charity case

I Never Thought I Would Be A Statistic

When they love you so much that you expressing
pain or disappointment become selfishness
When they love you so much that they use your past
and your weakness to remind you of You
When they love you so much only when the
conditions are right for them

CHAPTER 5

New Beginning

Just like the other stories like mine, the first time of abuse would not be the last time. That cycle continued for five years. For five long years I wore the face of the strong woman who could endure all. Under the make-up was hiding the black eyes and the bruises. Under the solemn face was laid the broken heart. Suicidal thoughts, guilt, and shame trickled down my face with each tear. I thought if I just listened to him, just enough, I could make it to the next day unharmed. I guess at some point I got so use to the abuse; I could just live through it as if nothing ever happened. I was able to turn his voice on and off like a switch. I would sit down and let him talk for hours without saying a word, and when the time came, I would let him use my body. I would lay there and wait for him to be done, and then afterwards roll over and fall asleep. But on the inside, deep inside, I was waiting for a Savior. A miracle. A way out.

I was so messed up that I got so used to my situation, and I could not even bear the thought of being alone or being without him. Somehow, he made me depend on him. The pain was normal like breathing, and it kept me from finding the courage to leave. Somewhere down the line he cheated again, which is how it usually goes, but he managed to convince me it was my fault. "If you were more loving, sweet, and understanding, I would not feel the need to have someone else." I really believed it was my fault. I sorted through my pain and decided to be a better wife.

Then, he got arrested. I remained a captive of my own feelings. I still helped him, and he came back home where I endured several more years of verbal, physical, emotional, and sexual abuse.

Nobody knew what was happening behind closed doors. They thought I was just suffering from depression; shown by my lack of sleep, my heightened anxiety, and my social isolation.

The fact of the matter is this: you can never know who around you is a victim and who is an abuser. Now, every day I think of how blessed I am to call myself a survivor because so many others did not get that chance. Even if I am still struggling with emotional instabilities and have to go to therapy, I am alive, and I have my healthy son. We have a chance to start over and that in itself is the best thing that has ever happened to me, to us in five years.

Finally, being able to enjoy the quietness of our home, and listening to the sound of only our breathing became a beautiful thing and my son and I were safe. My son's father recently took me back to court by trying to not pay child support. They actually decreased the amount that he had to pay weekly to support his son which was unbelievable to me. However, I found out afterward that this was common in these situations.

I believe the judicial system needs to be reformed, because I think that they do not give enough consideration to the victims of domestic violence especially if they don't have any recent police reports. They only consider facts that they can analyze, which is understandable, but they are also failing to see the bruises invisible to the human eye. Why are you forced to stand in a courtroom and face your abuser and his malicious ways just to prove a point? "Just be happy you made it," everyone says. But honestly, is that the best our society can offer to its survivors of domestic violence?

Today, despite all my insecurities, pain, hurt and suffering, I look at my son and I realize I must patch up my heart and move on. Bryant McGill said, "Your heart is not broken. Hearts don't break. What you are feeling is growing pains. Your heart is expanding in wisdom, compassion, and strength, so one day, you can love even more." I really love this quote. We all know it's easy to say, "I love you," but it takes a special kind of wisdom, compassion, and strength to continue to love after you have been hurt, betrayed, dismissed, manipulated, used, and lied to. Forgiveness is not optional.

After going through the stages of grieving and loss, I understood that in order to move on. I had to forgive myself. I realized to be free, I also had to forgive him and allow the God in me to reflect on the outside. I had to free myself from the guilt, the bitterness, and the resentment that had overtaken me. I did not want to be that woman carrying her past hurt everywhere she went while poisoning everything she touched. God opened my eyes to my issues and allowed me to find peace.

As long as I am breathing, it isn't over. Even if sometimes some tears leave furtively and silently from my eyes and roll down my cheeks, I couldn't stop pushing forward just because I think I am broken. I had to find a way to improve my mindset. I had to learn to let go of everything that was keeping me bound, stagnated, and sad. God offered me another chance in life and I had to take it and run with it. As life goes on, I know I will never be the same again because something inside my heart died, but I know that I am going to be ok. Embracing my pain is not a sign of weakness as I used to think. Sometimes we need to weep deeply and say goodbye in order to move forward freely. When moving on is for the better, being alone becomes more valuable and less frightening.

It is not the end. The love might have died, but you are not destroyed. You have to be open to: these long, cold, and lonely nights. These time-consuming days, these journeys toward the disarray and the realization that nothing really counted. Stop just hoping that you can change the situation. You have to be ready to walk in this ocean of fire.

When you are finally ready to let go there is no turning back. You have to be ready to take these extensive walks back and forth and stop questioning yourself. You must be ready to accept that your life and your dreams are not dead.

There was a time I was afraid to move on. When I finally accepted the fact that my old life was only an illusion, I had to make a decision. I had to open myself to the unknown. I was willing to start over and let go of the jealousy, the drama, the pain, the hurt, the discord, and the disappointments. I had to be strong. I realized that when the time comes, we have to be okay with the idea of letting go and letting God in order to reach the next step. We are all guilty of letting fear into our lives: fear of losing, fear of failing, fear of not being good enough, fear of the unknown. It is fine to be hesitant and nervous, but we should not let fear take over and paralyze us. We should not let doubt stop us.

So much happened in one year. It is crazy how you can look back and realize how much life has changed. The people who left, entered, and stayed in your life. The memories you will not forget and those you wish you did. Reflecting on how you have endured the pain, the hurt, the disappointment, the tears, the headaches, and the heartaches. Then, experiencing the joy, the happiness, the satisfaction, the achievements, the victories the fulfillment, and the endings, and the beginnings.

I am still learning, and I am still growing. On my road to recovery, I have discovered a lot about myself. I have realized how self-sufficient and how strong I could be. I can truly say that I am in a better place and I have made peace with myself. I still have to work on a lot of self-esteem issues, but now more than ever, I know it is possible. I can become what God has created me to be.

All this would certainly not be possible without the amazing people God placed in my life. Some, like Bryant McGill has said, were "for a season, some others for a reason and the rest for a lifetime." Yet, all participated actively in my journey of growth and self-discovery.

Furthermore, to everyone who was and is in an abusive relationship, I'd like to salute you.

Additionally, if no one has ever told you this, I would like to let you know that you are all so strong and so beautiful. You can overcome your insecurities. Be brave and embrace yourself. You can be the light you were meant to be; feed your spirit and nourish your soul. YOU ARE CALLED FOR GREATNESS.

Twenty-Four Seconds

One, two, three
I am falling for you
Four, five, six
I am in love with you

Seven, eight, nine
I am in your arms
Ten, eleven, twelve
The night feels so warm

Thirteen, fourteen, fifteen
The morning is here
Sixteen, seventeen, eighteen
You are already gone

I Never Thought I Would Be A Statistic

Nineteen, twenty, twenty-one
My tears are dropping
Twenty-two, twenty-three, twenty-four
My heart is breaking

CHAPTER 6

Articles

In order to improve my life, I had to improve my mindset. I had to understand that I had to come out of my shell and re-adjust to my new situation. In 2016, when I finally started talking about my story, I realized the number of human beings who shared a situation similar to, or worse than mine. I had to do something about it. At the time, I didn't have that many resources (still don't), but I had to figure out a way that I could help support survivors and possibly prevent others from ever experiencing what I did. I started researching and inquiring more on the subject.

In August 2016, *Beyond The Abuse* emerged out of a pursuit to inspire and support the community. In the pages that follow, there are articles I published; *Beyond The Abus*e's, Facebook page and due to their relevancies, I wanted to share them with you.

Article 1
Why Abused Victims Don't Speak Up?

We often ask ourselves why the victims of abuse don't say anything. We tell ourselves, "I wish he/she would have said something. If I would have known, I could have helped." The fact is we don't really know the struggles these victims/survivors are going through in their everyday lives, and the guilt they could be carrying for an action that they are not responsible for.

The Following are some of the main reasons why many victims/survivors remain silent and they are very complex:

- **Self-Blame**

Victims/survivors usually blame themselves because they think they are responsible for what is happening. They think they did something wrong. Sometimes, they even think they deserve the abuse they are receiving from the abuser.

- **Shame**

They are carrying a deep sense of shame. The thought of someone knowing their situation can be very devastating. It is so much easier to just deny the abuse and live life like everything is ok.

- **Fear**

One of the most obvious reasons is fear. The victims are fearing for their lives, their families and loved ones and their children in most cases. Some Abusers make victims feel powerless and dependent on them. At this point, talking doesn't become an option anymore.

- **Respect**

Our society has perpetuated the mindset that being fragile and traumatized is a sign of weakness. Being strong and tough are considered to be very admirable characteristics. In most cases, the perpetrators, besides having these admirable characteristics, are very friendly, easy-going, and respectable people. This often stops victims from coming forward.

It is very important to understand how hard it is for the victims and survivors to speak up. That's why we need to pay attention to the little signs and mostly listen to friends, family members, and coworkers who might happen to come to us for help. It is important not to dismiss, diminish or disregard their situation/story, because we must remember not all victims become survivors. Some never live long enough to be helped.

And most of all remember, if you or anyone you know need help or more information, don't hesitate to speak up. The hotline is free and confidential. Call 1-800-799-7233 if anything you've read brings any suspicion or doubt regarding your own relationship or that of someone you know.

First Published on August 20, 2016 on
https://www.facebook.com/Beyond-the-Abuse-2092353357655937/

Article 2
Children and Domestic Violence

About 3 to 4 million children between 3 to 17 years old are at risk of exposure to domestic violence every year and in most of the cases there are women victims of male partners involved.

These children witness the abuse on a regular basis and become fearful, worried, nervous, and concerned. They are always watchful and are waiting for the next incident to happen. Besides feeling unsafe all the time, they also are feeling worthless and powerless because they are unable to do anything to change their environment.

Nobody really knows what is going on inside of a child's head who witnesses abuse. They can become angry and carry feelings of shame, embarrassment, humiliation, and guilt. They can also isolate themselves.

Some of the signs and symptoms that a child might be exposed to some type of abuse include:

- Stomachaches and/or headaches
- Bedwetting
- Withdrawal
- Anxiousness to please
- Anxiety
- Poor attention which may result in poor school performance and attendance
- Increased aggression with peers or mother
- Low self-esteem

- Depression
- Self-injuring
- Thoughts of suicide

Children from violent homes are more prone to use alcohol/drugs, develop post-traumatic stress disorder, and become juvenile delinquents and engage in criminal activity later in life. It is also one of the main reasons why children run away.

We need to protect our children at all cost and break the cycle of violence.

Published on October 22, 2016 on
https://www.facebook.com/beyondtheabuse/

Article 3
Stop Empowering Abusers!

We would never think that a person in his or her right mind would consider empowering an abuser. Unfortunately, I found out that our society has accepted many customs and behaviors that are playing a part in the empowerment of abusers.

- One of them is our silence. Keeping quiet about an abusive situation that you might be aware of or might be in, doesn't help. It just gives the abuser the feeling that he can get away with everything. It makes him feel that he is untouchable.

- Another one is making excuses for his/her behavior. It has been proven that alcohol use, drug use, stress, and mental illness do not cause domestic violence; they may go along with the violence, but they do not cause it. These excuses are just used to rationalize an abuser's actions which are under no circumstances acceptable.

- Another one is referring partners to couples counseling. I was really surprised when doing my research, I learned about this. Social worker Susan Schechter says that couples counseling is "an inappropriate intervention that further endangers the victim…It encourages the abuser to blame the victim by examining her/his 'role' in his/her problem. By seeing the couple together, the therapist erroneously suggests that the partner, too, is responsible for the abuser's behavior."

- The last one I will mention in this article is how our society views the abuser and how this view remains unchanged even as seeing proof of abuse. Our society often says that a man who batters is often a good father and should have the right to have joint custody of their children if the couple separates. However, studies have found that men who batter their wives also abuse their children in 70% of cases. And even in the cases where the child wasn't directly abused, he/she suffers from witnessing one parent assault another. Batterers also manifest an increased interest in their children at the time of separation just to maintain contact/control over their partners.

    Let's not worsen the victim's pain and suffering, increase their feeling of hopelessness and helplessness by contributing to the empowerment of their abusers.

Published on August 24, 2016 on https://www.facebook.com/beyondtheabuse/

Article 4
Some Examples of Abusive Situations

In a domestic abuse relationship between intimate partners, one person seeks to assert power and control over the other one. The different types of abuse include physical, psychological, emotional, economic, and sexual abuse.

Some signs of physical abuse are: pinching, tripping, punching, grabbing, beating, pulling hair, slapping, shoving, biting, twisting arms, kicking, using a weapon against you, throwing you down, chocking, hitting, or pushing.

Psychological abuse signs include:

- Making or carrying out threats to do something to hurt you emotionally
- Threatening to commit suicide
- Threatening to take away the children or to harm them
- Threatening to harm the family of origin (for example, parents and siblings)
- Threatening to report you to a governmental agency (for example, the Internal Revenue Service and the Immigration and Naturalization Service)
- Threatening to harm pets or injuring or killing them

Emotional abuse signs are putting you down, making you think you are crazy or feel bad about yourself, playing mind games, treating you as if you are a servant and making all the big decisions, isolating and controlling what you do, or using your children as well to make you feel guilty or to harass you.

Economic abuse signs are: preventing you from getting or keeping a job, taking your money, making you ask for money, giving you an allowance, or controlling your finances in other ways.

Sexual abuse signs include: making you do sexual things against your will, treating you as if you are a sex object, or physically attacking the sexual parts of your body.

Remember if you find yourself in an abusive relationship, it is not your fault and you are not alone…

SPEAK UP – SPEAK OUT

Publish on May 9, 2017 on https://www.facebook.com/notes/beyond-the-abuse/some-examples-of-abusive-situations/2281363575421580/

ABOUT THE AUTHOR

Joanne M. Chérisma is a Haitian born writer, a born-again Christian, a mother. and a nurse by profession. She is also the author of *Une Vie Une Histoire.*

Her popular page, *Beyond the Abuse,* was created in order to bring awareness on abusive relationships and provide hope, empowerment, support, and confidence to the victims. Joanne writes poetic prose that speaks to the hearts of many. Her passion for writing embodies her empathetic nature while showcasing inner human vulnerability that sometimes goes unheard.

Joanne uses her writing as an outlet and voice for those who can understand the slings and arrows of life. She has a realistic view of situations which allow her readers to go on journeys through her writing. She lives in New York.

In *I Never Thought I Would Be A Statistic,* she shares her testimony of how she overcame an abusive relationship.

I NEVER THOUGHT I WOULD BE A STATISTIC

JOURNAL

I Never Thought I Would Be A Statistic

I Never Thought I Would Be A Statistic

I Never Thought I Would Be A Statistic

I Never Thought I Would Be A Statistic

I Never Thought I Would Be A Statistic

I Never Thought I Would Be A Statistic

I Never Thought I Would Be A Statistic

I Never Thought I Would Be A Statistic

I Never Thought I Would Be A Statistic

I Never Thought I Would Be A Statistic

I Never Thought I Would Be A Statistic

I Never Thought I Would Be A Statistic

I Never Thought I Would Be A Statistic

I Never Thought I Would Be A Statistic

I Never Thought I Would Be A Statistic

I Never Thought I Would Be A Statistic

I Never Thought I Would Be A Statistic

I Never Thought I Would Be A Statistic

I Never Thought I Would Be A Statistic

I Never Thought I Would Be A Statistic

I Never Thought I Would Be A Statistic

I Never Thought I Would Be A Statistic

I Never Thought I Would Be A Statistic

I Never Thought I Would Be A Statistic

I Never Thought I Would Be A Statistic

www.ingramcontent.com/pod-product-compliance
Lightning Source LLC
Chambersburg PA
CBHW052201110526
44591CB00012B/2029